new studio design

daab

Un estilo de vida más flexible, el alza del precio de los alquileres y el aumento de los hogares unipersonales han provocado, especialmente en las grandes ciudades, que las viviendas se limiten cada vez más a una sola estancia. No obstante, esto no tiene por qué suponer un inconveniente, ya que se puede aprovechar el espacio de forma óptima con un diseño inteligente; un equipamiento minimalista, muebles a medida y el predominio de colores claros son tres ingredientes básicos de cualquier estudio, en el que la premisa es prescindir de todo lo superfluo. A menudo, los apartamentos de dimensiones pequeñas disponen de poca luz natural; una solución para disfrutar de un estudio amplio y bien iluminado es colocar puertas correderas de plexiglás o vidrio acrílico y distribuir el espacio en varios niveles.

Un style de vie plus flexible, la hausse des prix des loyers et la croissance du nombre de maisons individuelles ont fait, spécialement dans les grandes villes, que les demeures se limitent toujours plus à une pièce unique. Cependant, cela ne doit pas constituer nécessairement un inconvénient. En effet, il est possible de tirer parti d'un espace de manière optimale grâce à un design intelligent ; un équipement minimaliste, des meubles sur mesure et la prédominance des couleurs claires sont trois ingrédients essentiels de tout studio, pour lesquels la prémisse est de se passer du superflu. Souvent, les appartements de dimensions réduites disposent de peu de lumière naturelle ; une solution pour jouir d'un vaste studio bien illuminé consiste à prévoir des portes coulissantes de plexiglas ou de verre acrylique et à distribuer l'espace en plusieurs niveaux.

Uno stile di vita più flessibile, l'incremento degli affitti e l'aumento delle famiglie unipersonali ha fatto sì che, specialmente nelle grandi città, le abitazioni si riducano sempre di più soltanto ad un unico ambiente. Ciò nonostante, questo fenomeno non presuppone alcun inconveniente visto che è possibile ottimizzare al massimo lo spazio mediante un design intelligente. Delle infrastrutture minimaliste, mobili realizzati su misura e il predominio di colori chiari sono tre ingredienti principali di qualsiasi studio, dove la premessa obbligatoria è prescindere da tutto ciò che è superfluo. Spesso, gli appartamenti di piccole dimensioni dispongono di poca luce naturale; una soluzione per poter godere di uno studio ampio e ben illuminato è sistemare delle porte scorrevoli in plexiglas o vetro acrilico e distribuire lo spazio in vari livelli.

Ein flexiblerer Lebenstil, steigende Mietpreise und die Zunahmen von Single-Haushalten haben gerade in den Metropolen dazu geführt, dass sich die Wohnfläche immer mehr auf einen einzigen Raum beschränkt. Dies muss allerdings kein Nachteil sein, da man durch ein intelliligentes Design den Raum optimal ausnutzen kann. Eine minimalistische Einrichtung, individuell angefertigtes Mobiliar sowie die Verwendung heller Farben sind für ein Studio besonders geeignet; gilt es doch auf alles Überflüssige zu verzichten. Oft verfügen kleine Apartments über wenig natürliche Beleutung. Eine Lösung für ein lichtdurchflutetes und geräumiges Studio besteht in der Verwendung von Plexiglas oder Acrylglas Schiebetüren und der Anordung des Raumes auf verschiedenen Ebenen.

A more flexible lifestyle, increasing rents and a greater number of single-person homes have all meant that apartments, especially in big cities, have been reduced to a single room. This does not necessarily have to be a disadvantage however. The use of space can be optimised with an intelligent design; minimalist amenities, made-to-measure furniture and predominantly light colours are three basic ingredients of any studio flat, where the premise is to do without all that is superfluous. Often, small apartments have little natural light; a solution to increase both space and the amount of light is to include perspex or acrylic glass sliding doors, and spread the space over different levels.

BEHF Architekten | Vienna, Austria
Seefels Apartment
Kränten, Austria | 2003

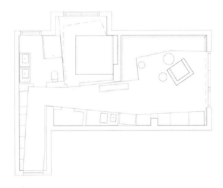

Beriot, Bernardini & Gorini | Madrid, Spain
All in One Piece
Madrid, Spain | 2002

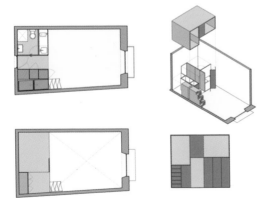

Casadesus | Barcelona, Spain
Loft You and Me
Barcelona, Spain | 2005

TU
YO
Si
No
- anar al cine
- menjar "xuxes"
la tele
de compres
tard
i beure
· fer el "vago"
- anar al gimnàs
- menjar verdures
fruita, peix,
llegums cereals..
- fer la compra
- anar de vacances
- arribar puntual
a la feina

Cassandra Komplex | North Melbourne, Australia
Chameleon Warehouse Extension
North Melbourne, Australia | 2003

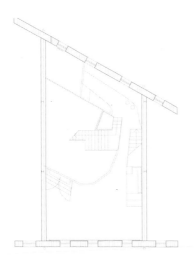

Estudio Cometalledo | Barcelona, Spain
Penthouse in Black and White
Barcelona, Spain | 2004

Feyferlik & Fritzer | Graz, Austria
Apartment Doppelhofer
Vienna, Austria | 2001

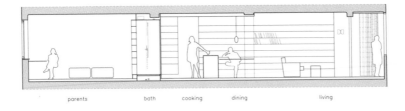

parents   bath   cooking   dining   living

Hobby A. | Salzburg, Austria
Nomad Home
Salzburg, Austria | 2005

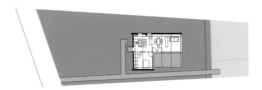

Javier Hernández Mingo | Madrid, Spain
Apartment Escorial
Madrid, Spain | 2002

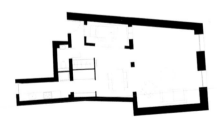

Luigi Colani | Karlsruhe, Germany
Rotor House
Oberleichtersbach, Germany | 2004

Minim Arquitectura Interior | Barcelona, Spain
Studio Marina Street
Barcelona, Spain | 2005

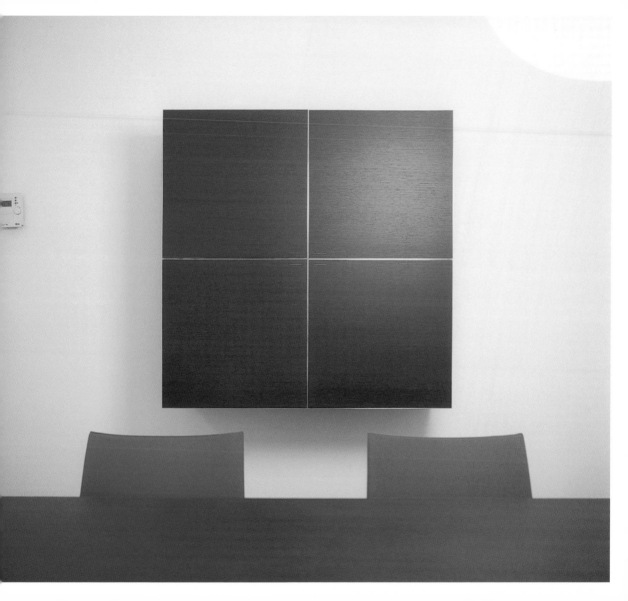

Peter Tyberghyen | Gent, Belgium
Apartment in Paris
Paris, France | 2005

Plasma Studio | London, UK
Loft for Videoartists
London, UK | 2003

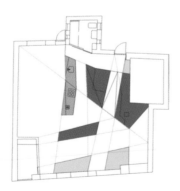

Raumteam 92 | Berlin, Germany
Loft Gerald S
Berlin, Germany | 2005

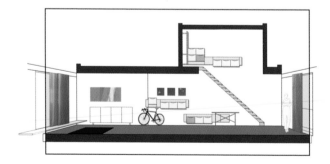

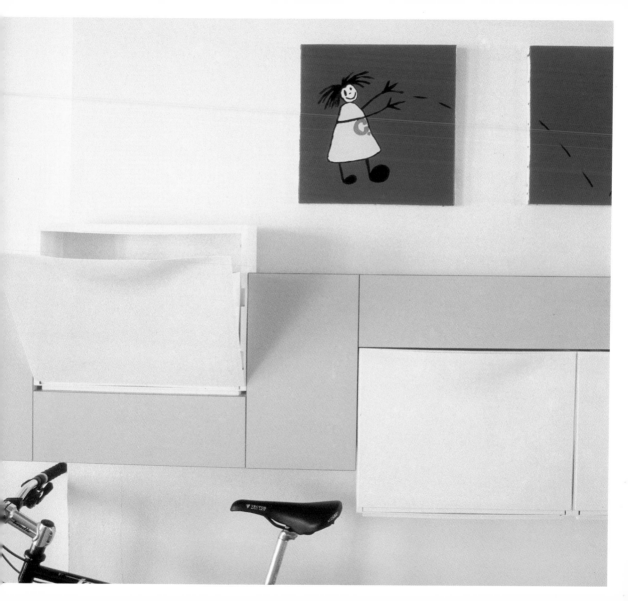

Roger Hirsch Architect, Myriam Corti | New York, USA
Home and Office for a Graphic Designer
New York, USA | 2002

Splitterwerk | Graz, Austria
Ivory Fresh Shell
Bad Waltersdorf, Austria | 2004

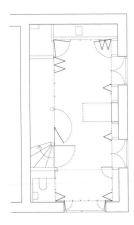

Stone Design | Madrid, Spain
Cutu's Home
Madrid, Spain | 2002

Studio Aisslinger | Berlin, Germany
Loftcube
Berlin, Germany | 2005

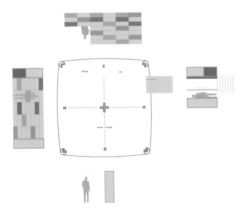

Studio Associato Bettinelli | Bergamo, Italy
Monolocal
Milan, Italy | 2004

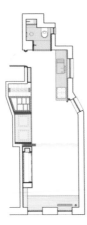

Studio Rodighiero Associati | Mantova, Italy
Flat in Castiglioni
Castiglioni delle Stiviere, Italy | 2004

Tang Kawasaki Studio | New York, USA
Nelson Residence
New York, USA | 2004

White Architects, White Design | Gothenburg, Sweden
Optibo
Gothenburg, Sweden | 2003

BEHF Architekten
Kaiserstraße 41, A-1070 Vienna, Austria
P +43 1 524 17 500
F +43 1 524 17 502
behf@behf.at
www.behf.at
Seefels Apartment
Photos: © Rupert Steiner

Beriot, Bernardini & Gorini
Maestro Alonso 22, local 6, Madrid, Spain
P +34 913 563 354
beriot-bernardini@arrakis.es
All in One Piece
Photos: © Ángel Baltanás

Casadesus
Verge del Pilar 2, 2-1, Molins de Rei, 08750 Barcelona, Spain
P +34 936 684 760
F +34 936 684 724
estudi@casadesusdisseny.com
www.casadesusdisseny.com
Loft You and Me
Photos: © Nuria Fuentes
Special thanks to Casa Decor 2005

Cassandra Komplex
51 O'Connell Street, North Melbourne VIC 3051, Australia
P +61 3 93 29 8308
F +61 3 93 29 8309
staff@cassandracomplex.com.au
www.cassandracomplex.com.au
Chameleon Warehouse Extension
Photos: © John Gollings

Estudio Cometalledo
Lledo 8, bajos, 08002 Barcelona, Spain
P +34 933 151 857
F +34 932 687 952
cometalledo@yahoo.com
Penthouse in Black and White
Photos: © Gogortza & Llorella

Feyferlik & Fritzer
Glacisstraße 7, A-8010 Graz, Austria
P +43 316 34 76 56
F +43 316 38 60 29
feyferlik@inode.at, fritzer@inode.cc
Apartment Doppelhofer
Photos: © Paul Ott, Graz

Hobby A.
Ignaz Härtl Strasse 9, 5020 Salzburg, Austria
P +43 662 641 152
F +43 662 641 993
hobby.a@subnet.at
www.hobby-a.at
Nomad Home
Photos: © Angelo Kaunat

Javier Hernández Mingo
Alameda 6 (local derecha), 28014 Madrid, Spain
P +34 914 297 774
F +34 914 290 821
tiri71@hotmail.com
Apartment Escorial
Photos: © Luis Hevia

Luigi Colani
Gewerbering 2-4, 76149 Karlsruhe, Germany
P +49 721 783 1988
F +49 721 783 1686
info@colani.de
www.hanse-colani-rotorhaus.de
Rotor House
Photos: © Hanse Haus

Minim Arquitectura Interior
Avda. Diagonal 369, 08037 Barcelona, Spain
P +34 932 722 425
F +34 934 883 447
info@minim.es
www.minim.es
Studio Marina Street
Photos: © Gogortza & Llorella

Peter Tyberghyen
Begijnhoflaan 45, 9000 Gent, Belgium
P +32 9 223 69 36
F +32 9 225 31 13
peter@tyberghien.de
Apartment in Paris
Photos: © Alejandro Bahamón

Plasma Studio
19 Mentmore Terrace, E8 3PH London, UK
P +44 20 8985 5560
F +44 871 2112 532
info@plasmastudio.com
http://plasmastudio.com
Loft for Videoartists
Photos: © Peter Guenzel

Raumteam 92
Wrangelstr. 92, 10997 Berlin, Germany
P +49 30 6162 9440
F +49 30 6162 9442
info@raumteam92.com
www.raumteam92.com
Loft Gerald S
Photos: © Stefan Meyer

Roger Hirsch Architect, Myriam Corti
91 Crosby Street, NY 10012 New York, USA
P + 1 212 219 2609
F + 1 212 219 2767
roger@rogerhirsch.com
www.rogerhirsch.com
Home and Office for a Graphic Designer
Photos: © Minh+Wass

Splitterwerk
Mandellstrasse 33, A-8010 Graz, Austria
P +43 316 810598
F +43 316 810598 40
splitterwerk@splitterwerk.at
www.splitterwerk.at
Ivory Fresh Shell
Photos: © Paul Ott, Graz

Stone Design
Cordón 10, 28005 Madrid, Spain
P +34 915 400 336
F +34 915 400 182
info@stone-dsgns.com
www.stone-dsgns.com
Cutu's Home
Photos: © Juan Merinero

Studio Aisslinger
Oranienplatz 4, 10999 Berlin, Germany
P +49 30 3150 5400
F +49 30 3150 5401
studio@aisslinger.de
www.aisslinger.de
Loftcube
Photos: © Steffen Jänicke

Studio Associato Bettinelli
Via Carrozai 6b, 24122 Bergamo, Italy
P +39 35 235 796
F +39 35 225 941
betinellistudio@bitbit.it
Monolocal
Photos: © Andrea Martiradonna

Studio Rodighiero Associati

Piazzale Resistenza 12, 46043 Castiglione D/S, Mantova, Italy

P +39 0376 63 8883

F +39 0376 67 1187

sra@sra.it

www.sra.it

Flat in Castiglione

Photos: © Antonio de Luca & Alessandro Lui

Tang Kawasaki Studio

338 East 5th Street #19, NY 10003 New York, USA

P + 1 212 614 9594

F + 1 212 614 9594

jason@tangkawasaki.com

www.tangkawasaki.com

Nelson Residence

Photos: © Bjorg Arnasdottir

White Architects, White Design

Magasinsgatan 10, Box 2502, 403 17 Gothenburg, Sweden

P +46 31 60 86 00

F +46 31 60 86 10

info@white.se

www.white.se

Optibo

Photos: © Richard Lindor

© 2006 daab
cologne london new york

published and distributed worldwide by
daab gmbh
friesenstr. 50
d‑50670 köln

p +49-221-94 10 740
f +49-221-94 10 741

mail@daab-online.com
www.daab-online.com

publisher ralf daab
rdaab@daab-online.com

creative director feyyaz
mail@feyyaz.com

editorial project by loft publications
© 2006 loft publications

editor anja llorella
layout luis f. sierra
english translation jay noden
french translation michel ficerai / lingo sense
italian translation maurizio siliato
copy editing alicia capel tatjer

printed in spain
gràfiques ibèria, spain

isbn 3-3-937718-76-1
d.l. B-29670-2006